Wata

Magic

WALTER JONES

Published by I.B.G. Publications, Inc., a Power to
Wealth Company

Web Address: WWW.IBGPublications.Com

admin@IBGPublications.Com / 904-419-9810

Copyright, 2021 by Walter Jones

IBG Publications, LLC, Jacksonville, FL

Jones, Walter
Wala Magic
WWW.WeRChange.org

ISBN 978-1-956266-02-3

Printed in the United States of America.

Dedication

I would like to dedicate this book to the youth of today and the future. It is my hope that this content will be motivational both now and forever!

Table of Contents

Acknowledgments

I would like to thank everyone on the IBG Publications Team. I would like to thank Coach Dr. Richelle McMillan for your guidance and reassurance through my publishing journey.

I would like to give a special thank you to Coach Audrea V. Heard for bringing my vision to life.

Thank you to everyone who was instrumental in leading me in the right direction, including Rebecca Givens. If it weren't for you being there at that moment in time, I would not be here today. There would be no book without the Author.

To my three loving children: Makaylah, Mahon, and Jalia Jones. I appreciate all your love and support!

My special thanks go out to the following:

- Mrs. Sylvia Brooks NSU academic advisor (school of business)
- Mr. Artie Williams (mentor of bad boys/troubled youth group while I was in high school)
- Mrs. Pat Kovas, Administrator of Bethel High School
- Minerva Douglas
- Carol Jones
- Mary Williams
- Walter Douglas
- Walter Jones Sr
- Andrea Michelle Kennard
- Deborah Kennard
- Senator Kaine
- Angela Brown
- Mildred Robinson
- Patrice Kennard
- Governor Northam
- Michael Lynch
- Claude Robinson
- The Nicholson Family
- Craig Breon

- Tracey Parker
- Devan Hill
- Glinda Sykes
- Johnny Sykes
- Way Veney
- David Olivis
- Congressman Scott
- The Lewis Family
- The Johnson Family
- Doris Mangrum
- Pete Adrian
- Carey Brown
- The Elam Family
- The Lynch Family
- Sgt. Jenrette
- Chief Drew
- Shawn Lynch
- Foley Jones
- Wayne Jones
- Joy Fauntleroy
- Wayne Veney
- Assistant Chief Gallop
- Butch Harper
- Marion Jones

- Troy Adams
- Fannie Brown
- Rashon Rogers
- Lance Jones
- Titus Sapp
- The White Family
- Carolita Jones
- Brandi Smedley
- Mercedes Mangrum
- Vee Frye
- Lt. Governor Justin Fairfax
- Robert Brown
- Robin Price
- Dr. Mason
- My Tucker Family
- The Peerman Family
- FRS Family

I can do all things through Christ which strengthens me. (NKJV)

-Philippians 4:13

Introduction

You will accomplish a lot and go through a lot in your lifetime. Life will teach you lessons you must learn to get you where you need to be.

You will not have to learn lessons if you gain wisdom from others' life experiences. Learn from their mistakes and triumphs: your path will be your own.

During my lifetime, it is my hope to inspire, motivate, and be more than just a sticky note in your brain. I want you to take these words everywhere you go and bury them in your spirit.

The definitions you find in this book have been defined by the Oxford Languages, Google, and Webster's Dictionary.

I hope you Enjoy!

Chapter 1

Never Stop

I always thought that dying young and in the flame of glory was the best way to leave this world. But the older I get, I realize that the best way to go out is old, surrounded by family and friends whom you love dearly.

When we depart this earth, we should strive to leave behind generational wealth and a path for the next generation to follow.

Never stop fighting and always look out for your family. Stop fighting with yourself, you got this!

You do not know it yet because you do not believe you do.

* * *

Denzel Washington, a great American actor, spoke to a group of college graduates during their graduation ceremony.

He said, "Early on in my career I auditioned for a part in a Broadway musical. I didn't get the job, but I didn't quit. Never give up and never stop fighting."

Denzel went on to win two Academy Awards®, two Golden Globe Awards®, the Screen Actors Guild Award®, the Tony Award®, many more awards and plenty nominations; all because he did not give up.

Do not stop when you fail, keep pushing towards your goals. Failure is a part of life, but quitting should not be an option. Keep growing, keep learning, and keep going!

* * *

Michael Jordan is without argument one of the greatest basketball players that has ever lived. Did you know he was cut from his high school basketball team?

After the hurt and pain of failing he did something about it. He kept practicing, working, and pushing himself harder.

He later became a 6-time NBA champion, 6-time NBA Finals Most Valuable Player, 10-time Scoring Leader, and 5-time NBA Most Valuable Player.

He was inducted into the Naismith Memorial Basketball Hall of Fame along with many other accolades and accomplishments. If he stopped when the going got tough, he would not be known as one of the greatest today.

Talk about impact!

The last year he played was 2003 and his line of sneakers, the 'Air Jordans' are still the top selling brand to date. Keep pushing and never stop, your dreams can become a reality.

Wala Magic Moment

"Change how you view yourself, your goals, and your future."
(Positive Vibes Only)

Your journey is just beginning! The clouds cannot stop the sun from shining. Continue to fight through any storm that comes your way.

You got this! Believe it because you do! You will come out on top of that mountain and shine brighter the next day, the next day, and the next day.

Never stop, your reward may be right around the corner. If you stop, all your time, effort, and work will be lost. You are powerful, you are strong, and you will make your ancestors proud.

The ones you love, respect, and cherish such as family and friends might think you're crazy. Value their opinion, but never feel crazy for believing in yourself and your dreams.

NOT believing in yourself is crazy. Listening to others' opinions about your dreams when they have not chased their own is crazy. Not putting in any effort into your dream is crazy.

You are not crazy; you are a visionary. Find your niche and be what you were meant to be!

Chapter 2
Time

Survival is defined as: the state or fact of continuing to live or exist, typically despite an accident, ordeal, or difficult circumstances (defined in the dictionary).

You are here alive and breathing in this very moment because you are a survivor. You can survive, you have survived, and you *will* survive.

Each time you survive your obstacle, hurdle, or trial you will come out ten times stronger than you were before.

I believe survival is where your strength, perseverance, and true grit lies. Don't *lose* time but gain knowledge and wisdom through time. In your lifetime, you will learn what to do so there will not be a next time for you or the next generation.

Time is defined by Google as: the continued sequence of existence and events that occur in an irreversible succession from the past. Time never stops and you cannot go backwards!

There are 365 days in a year and 24 hours in a day. It might sound like a lot of time, but it is not. Make the best of every second because you will not get it back.

This is your time! What will you do with it? Will you add to it or take away from it? Will you be a poison or a remedy? Will you allow life to beat you down or will you conquer it?

Wala Magic Moment

"This is your time! I know you can do it. Now believe you can. Your future aligns with the steps you take today."

If you do not use your time wisely you will miss your opportunity. By being present and available, when you make every day productive, you will become closer to where you want to be.

Cynthia Cooper-Dyke is an American basketball coach but started out as a great superstar player at the college of USC. She kept practicing her craft and practicing not knowing what the future could hold.

She had a vision, and it became a reality. In 1997 the WNBA (Women's National Basketball Association) was formed and in their first four seasons she was named the MVP! (Most Valuable Player)

Imagine if she did not use her time wisely to workout, study, and perfect her craft. Do you believe the outcome could have been the same? I do not think so and I believe you do not either.

You are a winner and winners do not procrastinate. Procrastination is the action of delaying or postponing because you do not want to do it at that time.

Missing assignments, always rushing, and burning

yourself out are *all* examples of poor time management.

Online Lucemi Consulting stated, "Effective time management means you take control of your time and energy. Taking control of your time enables you to achieve bigger and better results in less time, without the stress."

Doesn't that sound like something worth trying? What do you have time for? What you are willing to be available for is completely up to you. Use your time wisely; it is valuable.

Rapper and star Eminem from the movie 8 Mile said in the chorus to the song entitled 'Lose Yourself,' "You only get one shot. Do not miss your chance and blow this opportunity that comes once in a lifetime."

Do not allow opportunity to pass you by. Do not let those great gifts, talents, and hard work go to waste.

Will you take advantage of your opportunity or let it pass you by? Will you use effective time management or poor time management?

No one can value your time and take advantage of your time more than you can. Make every day count.

This is your season, and this is your time!

Chapter 3
Motivation

Think of your everyday life from start to finish. If you have goals and want to achieve those goals, you must possess motivation.

Motivation is defined as: the reason or reasons one has for acting or behaving in a particular way. I believe you cannot make it to the next level unless you're motivated to get there. The only way to get there is to take the necessary steps.

I have the word Motivation broken down by each letter. I also have the definition of the word. I am hoping it can help you in your journey as it has helped me in mine.

M-Meaning: what is meant by a word, text, concept, or ACTION.

O-Opportunity: a set of circumstances that make it possible to do something.

T-Tireless: having or showing great effort or energy.

I-Interest: the state of wanting to know about something or someone.

V-Value: the importance, worth, or usefulness of something.

A-Accomplish: achieve or complete successfully.

T-Training: the action of teaching a person or animal a specific skill.

I-Improve: make or become better.

O-Onward: towards a position that is a head of space.

N- Niffty: particularly good, skillful, or effective.

As an example of motivation, I would like to share some thoughts from people I truly respect. They took the time out to answer two questions I asked them. Their responses will help you become motivated and motivate others.

Question

1. *How has my community work with you been motivational for you?*

Answer

Christopher White (Engineer/Business Owner)

"It's motivational for me because it's inspiring. To know what you've been through and to see how far you've come, motivates and shows me it's not where you start from but how you finish that matters."

Question

2. What is Motivation for you?

Answer

Christopher White (Engineer/Business Owner)

"Motivation for me, is the spark that keeps the

29

dream and the drive going."

Question

1. *How has my community work with you been motivational for you?*

Answer

Ahmad Harmon (Assistant Maintenance Technician /Football Coach)

"Your community work has been motivational for me because of your desire to make a change in the area. You stand up for racial injustice and make sure everyone is treated fairly. The passion you have for the community is beyond motivational."

Question

2. What is Motivation for you?

Answer

Ahmad Harmon (Assistant Maintenance Technician /Football Coach)

"Motivation for me is positivity and integrity. I'm always motivated to do something when it's positive and done correctly when no one is watching."

Wala Magic Moment

"What is my motivation, you wonder?
My motivation is leaving an impact in this
world so great, my deeds will
last for eternity."

Chapter 4

You Are Somebody

Do you know what type of animal you would be if you lived in the animal kingdom, and had a choice?

Would you be a gazelle, an ant, a butterfly, or a lion? Nothing is impossible if you put your mind, body, and heart in it.

From the time your mom found out she was pregnant, to you breathing air in the delivery room, and even living and breathing today. You must believe you are stronger than you know because the truth is you are.

Wala Magic Moment

"You were born to be great! Roar as loud as you can! Your very existence is a miracle within itself."

If you think you are a nobody, then you're sadly mistaken. Change your way of thinking or you will fade in the shadows back to dust in the ground.

Hope for the best, wish everyone well, and show love for all. You cannot truly love someone else unless you love yourself first. Start by loving yourself, then you can be a blessing to someone else.

You are Somebody!

Like the song Lauren Hill sang in Sister Act II says, "If you want to be somebody and if you want to go somewhere you gotta wake up and pay attention!"

Believe in your dreams and set goals to obtain them. Evolution brings change but being ambitious should never change.

A human is a member of the species Homo sapiens, which means 'wise man' in Latin. Your wisdom should tell you that you are not a bum, you're not trash, and you're not useless. You are so much more. You are somebody!

The level at which someone or something

deserves to be valued or rated is *worth*. Know your worth because you are somebody.

Most people fail at trying to be something or someone they are not. Instead, focus on how well you can do in life being genuine. You are not insignificant, and this world is much more beautiful with you in it. Do not be afraid to be yourself because this is your best version of you.

No one can stop your destiny. Get away from negative energy and any energy detrimental to you and your growth. Negativity has no authority over your life.

You do not need a pat on the back or anyone's approval to make you feel like you're somebody. Do not be dependent on any of that. Be happy on the inside: you are powerful and not powerless. You are self-sufficient and not insufficient. You are here for a reason. Once you determine that reason you will see what you already know: you are somebody and you can be a blessing to someone else.

Chapter 5
Take Control

Learn to trust your gut and your instincts. Take control of the wheel and do not be a passenger watching all your dreams, future, and aspirations pass you by.

Be history or **make** history. You are unique and extraordinary. If you don't accept yourself, the world won't accept you.

Flaws and All.

You are already perfect in this circle of life, and

you are of excellent value. You decide if you are going to add to it or take away from it. Walk in your destiny and see how well you succeed at being who you are.

You must care about what you're doing, where you want to go and the person you want to become. If *you* do not, then why should anyone else care?

If an officer pulls you over for going too fast and writes you a ticket, who gets the ticket? The passenger or the driver? If you said the driver, you are correct.

Do not get distracted from what is important to you. Take control because you are liable and responsible for what you do in this life.

Wala Magic Moment

"Things worth fighting for like your beliefs, dreams, and goals do not come easy. If it did, everyone would try it and everyone would do it."

Each second you put in time and work, you get one step closer to achieving what you set out to do.

When you are mentally and physically exhausted, just smile and think about your end goal. Knowing where you are going and where you came from in your process should be enough to push you higher to the next level.

Remember: no number of excuses will get you to where you want to be. You must work extremely hard for it. Whether it be a game, test, rehearsal, practice, or competition.

Unbelievably, the work or lack of work you put in now will impact you later. Continue developing good habits now so your rewards can be much sweeter in the future.

Confidence, having passion about what you're doing, being responsible, and responsive are attributes of self-reliance.

Self-reliance is the ability to depend on yourself to get things done and meet your own needs. When you are self-reliant, you trust yourself and count on yourself!

There are many benefits of self-reliance but my favorite and most important is happiness. Your happiness depends on you because you control if you let yourself down or not.

It's all on you and nobody else. Trust yourself and your instincts. You got this!

Chapter 6
Don't Waste It

You could lose your innocence, your childhood, your valuables, your possessions, your friends, and loved ones. But you are still here for a reason.

Do not waste your life.

No more fighting with your inner self. No more hiding behind your true feelings or your true calling.

Wala Magic Moment

"You cannot knock on the door of opportunity if you don't take the first step towards the door."

Take advantage of the opportunity you have and do not waste it. My Aunt Patrice used to say, "People are starving all over the world. Don't waste your food."

I believe it is the same thing with life. You are not the only one in this world who wants more. You are not the only one who wants to be successful.

The word *waste* means to use or expend carelessly, extravagantly, or to no purpose. Your life has purpose and finding your purpose is too important to give up now, or just exist in this world. What will you do with your life and the time you have?

Strive to be legendary in everything you do although you do not know what the future may hold. But let me tell you, "Your future is bright beyond belief!"

Get everything you can out of life and learn something new every day. Don't be afraid to believe in yourself and your dreams. Be consistent in what you do so you will not just exist in this world, but you will *excel* in it.

Life is hard when you make it hard. Keep shining through your great works, honorable deeds, patience, and persistence.

Remember: you cannot genuinely appreciate winning if you have never lost. You may fall on your path, but by nature, you will get back up.

Do not ever give up! Your life is in your hands and that is enough to fight for. Every day is a new day to be better and another opportunity to be great!

Time waits for no one. It may move slow when you are bored or fast when you're having fun. But it never stops. Life only moves forward, and you can never go backwards.

Make the best of life every second of the day. Your life has meaning, your life has worth, and the greatest gift in this world is you!

Wala Magic.

ABOUT THE AUTHOR

Walter Jones

Walter Jones was born in Mobile, Alabama and raised in Hampton/Newport News Virginia (The Peninsula District). A graduate of Bethel High School, he obtained his Bachelor of Science degree in business management from Norfolk State University.

To assist in reducing the spread of COVID-19, Mr. Jones founded a disinfectant service and within the same year, launched the organization, We Are Change, LLC. He is the CEO of the company and assists in the branding, marketing, and fundraising efforts to expand the brand. We Are Change, LLC provides community resource fairs for youth and underprivileged community members.

Mr. Jones moves about the community through networking with the *NAACP*, *Organize Hampton*, and the *Newport News Police Department*. He continues his efforts to improve his community with unity marches throughout the city, voter registration sign ups, neighborhood, and cemetery cleanups.

As a spokesperson for We Are Change, LLC, Mr. Jones promotes unity through community discussions with political figures such as Governor Northam, and Congressman Bobby Scott. In addition to these efforts, he has organized several community events for the Lieutenant Governor Justin Fairfax along with serving as the campaign leader for Hampton Roads, also called the 'Peninsula Supporters.'

Mr. Jones is the proud father of three children: Makaylah Jones, Mahon Jones & Jalia Jones. He resides in the Virginia area where he proudly serves his community.

Made in the USA
Middletown, DE
08 February 2025

70613944R00031